A Positive
PRINCESS

Arts Pelago
Press

Coloring Dreams
For Inspiring Queens

"Empower yourself with education, strength, and confidence. You have the power to create your own destiny."

"Your attitude determines your direction."

- Unknown

"You are never too small to make a difference." - Greta Thunberg

"Embrace your uniqueness:
the world needs your originality to shine."

"The most beautiful thing you can wear
is confidence in your own uniqueness.

"The best way to predict the future is to create it." - Peter Drucker

"The future belongs to those who
believe in the beauty of their dreams."
- Eleanor Roosevelt

"The only person you are destined to become
is the person you decide to be.
Choose greatness."

"Dream big, work hard, stay focused, and surround yourself with good people." - Channon Rose

"Your uniqueness is your magic."
– Unknown

Made in United States
Troutdale, OR
05/04/2024

19646310R00046